From God, with Love

Finding Peace Within

Melissa A. Rivers

Published by Victorious You Press™
Charlotte NC, USA

TITLE: FROM GOD WITH LOVE
First Printed: 2024
Editor: Shay Oakley
ISBN: 978-1-959719-38-0
Printed in the United States of America

For details email joan@victoriousyoupress.com
or visit us at www.victoriousyoupress.com

"If it is possible, as far as it depends on you, live at peace with everyone."

Romans 12:18 NIV

Dedication

This book is dedicated to the beautiful women, past and present, of the Rosehill Community in Kannapolis, North Carolina, who played an integral part in shaping my character.

My mom, Robin Taylor; my great-great grandma Irene Caldwell; my great grandma Alice Truesdale; my grandma Ruthie Norman; my great-great aunt Della Wilson; my great aunts Leo Hillman and Velma Wright; my aunts Gail Funderburke and Judith Cowan, Mrs. Ophelia Thomas and Mrs. Katherine Anthony.

Thank you for being actual examples of love.

The guidance that you imparted in my life will always remain strong.

Contents

Marriage & Family

Inspired by My Daughter Kyla

A Grandma's Love

Survivorship & Redemption

Foreword
Chantel Grier

Melissa was the first person I clung to when I started working in a new department. It was easy, as she had such a kind heart; she was warm and inviting. There was an incredible aura in her presence and it calmed my spirit, especially coming from a season in which I needed it. Upon meeting her, I do not believe she knew the power, balance, and beauty she possessed in helping others heal.

Whether personal, corporate or as a fellow entrepreneur, I've found Melissa to be gifted in helping people spiritually maneuver through the seasons of their lives. I am reminded of Maureen Brown Clark's "Sovereign God," a song that Melissa provided to reassure me of God's forever trusting hand during challenging times. Even in her battles with different life events, she's found it in her heart to show up for friends, family, colleagues, students, cancer patients and survivors. Melissa thrives in healing her community.

From God, With Love is a true testament to how Melissa has navigated through life and continues to pour into others. It serves as a reason to revisit its scriptures, poetry, and questions to challenge where you currently sit in life and how to find freedom in your experiences.

Introduction

Dear Woman of God,

It is time that you make peace with yourself. You are a purposeful and deliberate creation of God. You have been crafted and created with precise detail. Nothing about you is a mistake.

If you've lived long enough, you've experienced things that have been difficult to recover from. You've had your share of tearful nights where you've prayed for a solution to seemingly endless battles.

Life can hand you a fist full of sorrow and a heart full of hurt.

However, God is concerned about your state of mind. Your feelings matter to Him and He is genuinely interested in those issues that concern you. Remember in the book of Genesis, God visited Adam in the cool of the evening. The same love that was extended to Adam is available to you.

Every battle and struggle we contend with has already been settled in Heaven.

I pray that you use God's word to achieve success, peace, and empowerment in your daily life. May this book serve as an instrument for you to pray the Word of God and not pray your worries to Him. May you be enlightened to understand that God has given you power and dominion to overcome those things that hinder you. May you walk in deliberate authority by commanding your circumstances according to God's perfect will for your life.

Peace and Wellness,
Melissa

Inspiration

What Inspires Me

"O woman of God, your life is filled with challenges and victories, smiles and tears. You are a careful blend of life's many spices. Your personality is made up of so many different things, years of knowing you will not reveal everything that makes you who you are." (Jakes 2003)

I've always found peace in writing from as far back as I can remember. It was my first love. Growing up, I was determined to study journalism in college and travel the world, writing for various major magazines but I allowed life to get in my way.

As a little girl, I would create stories and scenarios in my mind of far-off places and wondrous adventures. It only took one word to get my mind spinning. In elementary school, I was known as the whiz kid who scored perfect on her writing tests. In the fourth grade, I ordered my free copy of the Constitution from Judge Wapner of the People's Court. When I received it, I was so amazed by the quality of the paper that it was printed on. It was off-white linen paper that felt important. I felt honored to have a personal copy. The feel of those pages between my fingertips further ignited my passion.

Through the years, life has taken me in all sorts of directions. I never realized my desire for journalism or traveling the world to freelance for magazines. The one thing that has remained constant in my life is my passion for writing. This passion has guided me through life's ups and downs.

Writing has served me well over my lifetime. I've used it to encourage new mothers, celebrate new brides and support grieving friends. I also turned to writing as a method of healing after experiencing breast cancer. The most rewarding experience I've received from writing is a closer walk with Jesus. Writing has become my form of prayer, a place of peace and a gift of purpose.

I am so thankful that God chose me to be a vehicle of expression through writing.

Jeremiah 20:9 (NIV)

But if I say, "I will not mention him or speak anymore in his name, "his word is in my heart like a fire, a fire shut up in my bones. I am weary of holding it in indeed, I cannot.

Inspiration

This gift you have given me, I cannot take this for granted

Years of molding and shaping me on fertile soil, it was
planted

Your whispers are so sweet; they fill my heart with
inspiration

One mention of your sovereign name and I get motivation

Your Word is hidden so deep in my heart

My mind begins to wonder, and my pencil will start

Dictating the thoughts that you bring to my mind.

Your Love for me is genuine, always caring and so kind

I am proud to spread the word about my dear Savior

I am humbled and grateful to walk in favor

If I were unable to write about His ways

My mind would ponder on how to fill my days

Lost without you would be my banner

So thankful am I not to live in this manner

Lessons
From My Daddy

Internal Dialogue

As life presents various challenges, it is essential to understand how your internal dialogue was formed. Past hurts and painful experiences are essential in helping to shape your self-image and your perception of the world. With a clear foundation of who you are in Christ Jesus, it's possible to understand who you were created to be.

Get to know you:

Take a few minutes to answer the following questions to better understand how you view yourself.

1. What is your most painful experience?
2. Are you holding on to any guilt from this experience?
3. Have you made peace with this situation? If so, how?
4. What do you enjoy doing?
5. Describe yourself using the first four adjectives that pop into your mind.

The Yellow Envelope

My daddy died when I was two years old. My brother and I would receive a yellow envelope every month containing funds to help my mother provide for us. Each month, I would eagerly await the arrival of the yellow envelope. If there was a delay in receiving it, I would get upset until it was delivered. For me, the Yellow Envelope served as a reminder that my daddy was still taking care of us long after his death and absence here on Earth. Each month, I would run to the mailbox excited to touch that yellow envelope with my daddy's name on it. I would read his name aloud and daydream about how much better my life would be if my daddy were still living. When I reached the age of 18, the yellow envelopes stopped coming. I still remember that sense of sadness I felt, knowing that the monthly meetings at the mailbox, daydreaming about my daddy, were coming to an end.

Once I released my dependence on receiving the envelope, I learned that God wanted me to depend on Him just as much. Through various transitions in life, He taught me how to trust in Him for everything. I soon learned that HIS blessings were not limited to a monthly meeting with a yellow envelope and that HIS provisions are forevermore.

My daddy's absence allowed me to understand the presence of God more clearly in my life. Those monthly meetings at the mailbox turned into daily walks with God.

I thank God for my daddy and the lessons I learned through the yellow envelope.

Inspired by: John 11:4 (NIV)

When he heard this, Jesus said, "This sickness will not end in death. No, it is for God's glory so that God's Son may be glorified through it."

A Father's Love

How could she have known that she would never see him
again?

Hear his words, feel his touch, or walk with him hand in
hand.

Hours passed as she waited in hopes that he would come

Days later, still no daddy, and she felt so all alone

The church was packed, and all who had come were full of
gloom and despair

Her cute little dress, frilly little socks, and, yes, her daddy
was there.

She looked at him and wondered why he was not looking
back

She cried out with emotion from that first pew where she
sat.

Daddy, wake up! Daddy, wake up!

But Daddy continued to sleep.

She continued to cry and scream with pain, and those seated in the church began to weep

As the lamp went dark and the casket was sealed

A new chapter in life, God began to reveal

A time of chaos and confusion, so surreal but not an illusion

This small little girl is alone in a world without her daddy!

Heart full of Love-Heartache: Long walks she began to take.

Promises made- Promises were broken: Strength and resilience would be her token.

Heart full of sorrow- Continuous prayer: On her knees, she fell into the arms of her Father, and on that day

The Holy Spirit met her and gently led the way.

Her first step was denial as she waited by the window; days passed, and she asked when was her daddy coming home.

As her Mama bravely told her daddy had gone away, she went back to the window and waited to see his face.

Her second step was anger; for a girl so young, this was danger. As she grew only a few relationships she knew.

Men would come, and men would go, but real Love she would never know because her heart still felt the anger that she knew from age 2.

Step three involved bargaining when she aged enough to realize. Living wasn't easy, and her worth was belittled in society's eyes.

Maybe God would take her too if only he knew all the pain she had endured through the years as she matured.

Depression was her next step, and it lasted a good while; bad decisions, a college dropout, and single mother filled her file.

Her final step was acceptance as she began to change her mind, yes Daddy died, but Jesus lives, and His spirit does remind

His Love will never fail, and His Grace removed the veil

Jesus lives, and she does, too

And her life is so brand new!

A Woman's

Desperation

Dear Lord,

Give me discernment in those matters of my heart. Keep me close to you and out of harm's way. Help me to understand the difference between man's agenda and your plans for me. Give me a deeper understanding of your decrees so that I may understand the purpose that you have given me. May I hear your voice when you speak to me, and may I never grow weary of serving you. May I always walk confidently, knowing how much you love me and show me how to reciprocate that love to others. May every work that I do receive your blessing.

I love you.

In Jesus' Name, I pray.
Amen

Genesis 3:6-7 (NIV)

When the woman saw that the fruit of the tree was good for food and pleasing to the eye, and also desirable for gaining wisdom, she took some and ate it. She also gave some to her husband, who was with her, and he ate it. 7 Then the eyes of both of them were opened, and they realized they were naked; so, they sewed fig leaves together and made coverings for themselves.

"O Desperate Woman"

O Desperate woman to become so wise

You gave up eternity because of your eyes

A pleasant sight you thought you had perceived

But foolish you, how easily deceived

The serpent came and sold you his plan

To shame humanity and curse the land

A close walk with God is what you lost

Before that bite, did you estimate the cost

Your sorrow was multiplied, and your husband shall rule

To work the ground and tend to it became his daily duel

But in your rebellion, God put His plan to work

A Savior set on redemption would be Earth's biggest perk

To save humanity from sin and shame was His mission

To educate the people and bring in the addition

Jews and Gentiles are all welcome, and God wants us all

To reap the benefits of redemption after humanity's fall

Grace and Mercy cover God's people from head to toe

Jesus is the only Saving Grace; soon, all the world will know.

Honest Prayers

The Gifts Found in Prayer

When you pray, do you pray your worries to God or do you pray God's word back to Him?

As stated in the Bible, God's word is alive and active. Out of habit, we may pray our worries, hoping to move God into action on our behalf sooner rather than later.

God has already considered every situation and circumstance that we could face. Take a second, go to the word, and pray God's word back to Him. Then, sit back and marvel at how He responds to His word. As the Bible says, "So shall my word be that goeth forth out of my mouth: it shall not return unto me void, but it shall accomplish that which I please, and it shall prosper in the thing whereto I sent it Isaiah 55:11 (KJV)."

Take a few minutes to create a one-of-a-kind, original *Prayer of Honesty* for yourself. Not only will it please God, but you will move closer to His presence.

Inspired by: Matthew 26:36 (NIV)

Then Jesus went with his disciples to a place called Gethsemane, and said to them, "Sit here while I go over there and pray."

A Prayer of Honesty

My dearest Heavenly Father

I hope I am not a bother

But from you, I need to hear

Just to know that you are near

I need to feel your love

And strengthened from up above

My issues have me, weary Lord

And I need to see more clearly

Your word to me revealed

In your presence, I am healed

I am in my sacred place

Lying prostrate on my face

I am putting aside the weight

You promised me you would take

I am casting my cares on you

Because your instruction tells me to

Lean not to my own understanding

Although my life can be demanding

I will have faith to trust and believe

That your promises will be achieved.

Marriage & Family

Ruth 4:14 (NIV)

The women said to Naomi: Praise be to the Lord, who this day has not left you without a kinsman-redeemer.

A Moment
Called Suddenly

In a moment called suddenly, God's vision was revealed

A request that I made known to Him, according to His will

I prayed for the divine release of a love that would not cease

I prayed to be covered and protected, no longer having my
love rejected

I prayed for favor and honor, realizing that I could no
longer

Be subjected to a lesser love than God's best sent from
above

He answered me so clearly; the love I longed for came near

So gentle was his hand, Lord, could this be the man

Standing right before my eyes and much to my surprise

Your vision did reveal that the love I longed for was real

With the bright moonlight on that perfect night

He dropped to one knee and proposed to me

His emotions were raw; the Grace of God is what I saw

Sounding like a testimony, there's no way this could be phony

His ministry was redemption, and God sent him on this mission

Dearly beloved, do you thee wed; ring on my finger and veil on my head

The crowd was gathered and waiting in awe; a covenant exchange is what they saw

Atonement was the theme of that day; my kinsman-redeemer took the shame away.

Inspired by My
Daughter Kyla

In My Daughter's Eyes

In my daughter's eyes, there are goals to achieve

There's a future to create and a legacy to leave

In my daughter's eyes, her life is like a song

And she's swaying to the beat of a song she made her own

In my daughter's eyes, the finish line is close

She excels at what she does, and she achieves more than
most

In my daughter's eyes, education is the way

To finance her dreams and to see a brighter day

In my daughter's eyes, I empower her to be

A woman full of confidence, grace and mercy

In my daughter's eyes, love makes her feel safe

I raise her with my love and I pour out my faith

Into a little girl so sweet, My Heavenly Father allowed me
to meet

Thank you, God, that I see love in my daughter's eyes!

A Grandma's Love

The Older Women Must Train the Younger Women to Love

When I was growing up, five generations of women helped raise me. I remember as a little girl calling for mama and 7 of the most beautiful faces would all turn to look in my direction. That's just how it was in my family. Those were the days when young women wanted to learn from the older generation. Everyone would show up to one central location just to sit, talk, laugh, and create good memories.

My most significant influence came from my great-great grandma, "Mama Caldwell." As a teenager, I would sit with her while my Aunt Lee went to work or to run errands. I loved it when no one else was home but us. Mama Caldwell could not walk on her own, so she was very dependent upon me. I would brush her hair, help her get dressed, and make sure she put on her powders and Chantilly perfume each day. She had the most amazing smell. She always wanted to wear her pearl ear tips and her outfit just wasn't complete without a tissue in her jacket pocket, and a pack of Juicy Fruit chewing gum. She was so dignified and full of love. Her willingness to allow me to help her instilled the gift of service to others within me.

Ladies,

We must return to that Titus 2:4 (NLT) kind of love, which says "These older women must train the younger women to love their husbands and their children."

Without someone leading the way, we are all destined to fail. Who will you take responsibility for and how will you impart your knowledge to the next generation?

Take a few minutes and list five ladies you can mentor in faith.

1. _____

2. _____

3. _____

4. _____

5. _____

Inspired by my great, great grandmother,

"Mama Caldwell"

A Lesson in Love

As we arrived at the hospital, my heart was full of sorrow.

Not knowing if my grandma would live and be with me tomorrow.

Reluctant to enter but wanting to go,

all the time God telling me there's something I need you to know.

The door was very heavy, as if opening a vault,

secrets were unlocked, and the answers that I sought.

Her face was full of love, and poised with grace,

she patted the bed for me to take my place.

I looked into her eyes and kissed her on her cheek,

She knew that I had come with a need to seek.

Exhausted from emotion, I could not stay awake,

I fell into a deep sleep as her last breath she began to take.

In a suddenly moment, God woke me with His love,

He wanted me to look in the corner up above.

A radiant light from far away came to greet

my grandma with open arms and her Savior she did meet.

A warm and inviting light filled the room,

I began to celebrate and did not feel the gloom

of losing my grandma because I felt safe

she wanted me to know Him and hold a sacred place

forever in my heart of that very day

when Jesus showed up and took all her pain away.

My grandma lived for a very long time. God showed her grace until the age of 99. Unable to walk and take care of her needs, she trusted me with those very private deeds. I loved to brush and comb her hair and a fresh pan of cornbread, she knew I would be there! A pack of Juicy Fruit was always in her pocket, her pearls and earrings, and sometimes her locket. She loved to sit in her favorite chair on the front porch, she would sit and stare at how the world was changing each day, knowing that Jesus was on His way.

Finding Me

When I married my husband, divorce was the furthest thing from my mind. I had never even considered the thought that my marriage would not last. Here I was, only six months in and contemplating divorce. How could this be? It felt so perfect and right in the beginning.

What I didn't know then, was that my need to feel safe and vindicated from past hurts led me to make an irrational decision about love. Losing my father at such a young age, coupled with the heartbreaks from old loves, left me feeling anxious to be chosen.

If only I realized sooner that God had been choosing me all along.

It's often said that if you look hard enough, you will find purpose in all things. I believe this is true.

The purpose that I found in my divorce was me. I found the purpose to live, love, and let go.

If you've ever been through a divorce, my prayer is that you learn to love yourself again, intently and intensely.

You've Got to Be More Careful

You knew I had to leave to find myself again

I was in a place where I felt lost, and confusion had set in

Things changed so quickly for me; within the blink of an eye

I thought I was prepared but soon found out that was a lie

The representative that I wed no longer showed genuine love

I felt betrayed and misled; I assumed I was far above

The traumas from my past and attracting hurtful things

But I was not, and here I am, disappointed but remembering

I can dwell in your shelter and find genuine rest

You are my refuge and my mighty fortress

You saved me from the snare and guarded me with your shield

A thousand may fall, but me, you chose to heal

Healed by your love and covered by your grace

No more weeping or crying. You dried the tears from my
face

You rescued me and restored my mind

I will honor and praise you with all of my time

Inspired by: Genesis 4:25 (NKJV)

"For God has appointed another seed for me..."

Another Chance

Like a stream of rushing water, you've been running from your past

You consider yourself weak and un-equipped for the task

You believe your life is over, and you've thrown in the towel

You have folded your arms and given up for now

You say it's way too hard and certainly not worth the pain

You've been walking around in circles, and your living has been in vain

Most days, your mood is sad, lonely, or depressed

You think that no one sees you, and they could not care less

But early one morning, as the new dawn breaks

The dew settles slowly, and HIS manna fills your space

The barren ground where you once stood

Reveals specks of green growth, so the soil here is good

God has appointed another seed just for you

Another hope, another opportunity, another chance to start brand new

For He sees you and considers all the pain that you feel

He heard your cry; He longs for your laugh, and He weeps because your issue is real

The issue is sin, and it keeps us bound

It cancels out faith and welcomes fear to hang around

It steals our confidence and keeps us trapped

It muffles our testimony and holds us in lack

It spoils our relations and curses our generations

It keeps us divided and un-united as nations

But God has appointed another seed just for you

Consider this verse and help spread the good news too

It's not too late to start fresh and realize

Your worth is grand and you are valuable in His eyes

Long before your birth, God knew you and called you His own

He formed you and created you with a purpose to be made known

Don't give up on yourself, and let His Word guide your path

Your struggle was not in vain and soon again, you shall laugh

For God has appointed another seed just for you

I can't wait to see you smile again and witness your testimony, too!

Survivorship & Redemption

Stay Close to Anything That Makes You Glad to Be Alive

As a breast cancer survivor, I've chosen to eliminate many things in my life. Negative stress, over-commitment, and a people-pleasing persona, just to name a few. In 2015 when I was diagnosed with cancer, there were so many other things that were going on with me. I had recently finalized a divorce while being promoted to a new position at work. I was raising my teenage daughter while looking forward to new beginnings after several consecutive years of hardship. My life was a huge contrast and just as I thought things were taking a turn for the better, a positive cancer diagnosis inserted itself into the mix.

I would like to say that my initial thoughts were that of concern for my health and how it would be affected. However, I am sad to admit that as a single mother and sole provider, my initial thoughts were riddled with concern over the amount of work that I would miss due to doctor visits and associated appointments. I tried to remain calm and upbeat on the outside while internally battling with thoughts of fear and stress. How would I make it? Who will take care of my daughter if I die? What does my diagnosis mean? Will I fully recover?

I praise God daily that I made it through that tumultuous time in my life. After the diagnosis, surgery, treatment, and recovery, I began sharing my story and immersing myself in the supportive community of breast cancer survivors and thrivers. I often reminded myself of the following: *"It is essential that you take care of yourself."* The more I focused on self-care and healing, the more my community of friends and supporters expanded. I began mentoring other women who were experiencing compounded challenges similar to mine. This simple act of sharing and engaging fueled my desire to live on purpose, share my story and encourage others.

My message to women who are overly committed to everything and everyone other than caring for themselves is as follows:

Do not neglect your physical health or your overall well-being.

You are so much more than your work, the family you care for, and

the service you provide in your community. Your accomplishments should be honored but in addition to these things, you are uniquely and wonderfully made; a chosen people, redeemed from all that attempts to hinder you. You were chosen to be alive for such a time as this.

When obstacles attempt to obscure the essence of who you are, stay close to the things that give you life! God gives you life.

Allow Him to be your refuge and your fortress; dwell in His shelter and watch

and wait as He commands His angels concerning you.

Rest in the assurance that God loves you and knows you by name.

He will protect you in times of trouble.

Breathe and enjoy living your life, for those who wait upon the Lord shall renew their strength. They shall run and not be weary. They shall walk and not faint.

My combined journeys through divorce, breast cancer, and unemployment were the springboard that helped me to find my purpose and launch my company. Origins of Peace, LLC, is where I provide coaching and consulting services to women who want to reduce stress and overwhelming feelings in their daily routine, by identifying opportunities to add more peaceful moments into their lives.

My company motto is, *"You Cannot Find Peace in A Place That You Do Not Trust."* Trust that you know exactly what's needed to live a more peaceful life. Identify those things and keep them close!

Peace and Blessings,
Melissa

2 Kings 8:6 (NIV)

The king asked the woman about it, and she told him. Then he assigned an official to her case and said to him, "Give back everything that belonged to her, including all the income from her land from the day she left the country until now."

Give It All Back

Before I got the news, you said I would be okay

The comfort you provided helped me make it through each day

As I journeyed through each stage, your compassion was so clear

I clung to every word you spoke, and I kept your scripture near

As a daily reminder to never give up, I always said my prayers

A few close friends, some are angels now, showed they really cared

When I rang that bell, it was the sound of restoration

When I rang that bell, I rang with high expectation

When I rang that bell, my life became different

I was finely free to live authentically

Your word said to live, and that's precisely what I did

No more playing small or having no voice at all

I decided to make choices that would help me prosper

I chose a plant-based diet and a peaceful mindset I did
foster

I am blessed to live cancer-free

I am blessed that you decided to *give it all back* to me

2 Timothy 2:20 (NIV)

In a large house, there are articles not only of gold and silver but also of wood and clay; some are for noble purposes, and some for ignorable purposes. If a man cleanses himself from the latter, he will be an instrument for noble purposes, made holy, useful to the master, and prepared to do any good work.

Made Useful

Rejection and heartache, intense lessons were learned

My smile was often hidden because emotions were burned

With a need to feel love and make the hurt go away

I was longing for that sacred place to rest and stay

But God saw my struggle and covered me with grace

He came to me one morning and put glory on my face

A glory so bright and a future new to me

Some cannot believe the sin that once consumed me

But now I am brand new, cleansed and ready for use

The yoke that had me bound is no longer a noose

To profess HIS word and HIS love to a chosen people

Who are hand-picked by God and all are loved equal

Holy, useful and prepared for good work

I'm accepting the commission to be one of God's clerks

The work is plenty but the workers are few.

Allow Him to cleanse you and become useful too.

Inspired by Genesis 29:17

A Poem for Leah

Recognize

Do you not know? Have you not heard?

God is the final word.

And His lasting decree spoken over me

A woman of radiance, love and beauty

I'm established by the power released from His right-hand

I have unlocked potential to achieve more than most can

For my reach is far greater than many have seen

I'm secure in myself with high self-esteem

My worth is far greater than rubies and gems

I'm talented, I'm confident and I'm liberated from within

My community is important to me; I encourage those in need

To live a better life and my advice, I pray they heed

Live up to your potential and never settle for less than the best

Show up for every challenge and deliver nothing less

Offer all you have to give, and your dreams will be fulfilled

Build your life on God's foundation and your future will be
sealed

Accept the blessings from His promise and make an oath to
live His way

Grasp the beauty in each moment and always seize the day!

Journal Pages for From God with Love

Life can come at you fast. In this book, we've visited a full range of situations and emotions that might cause you to reflect on the things you have experienced. The following journal pages are provided to allow you to assemble and document any thoughts about this subject matter.

Woman of God, for you are the salt of the Earth. May you walk in dignity and self-assurance, fully aware of your worth. May God continue to shine His face upon you, and may you continue to recognize His voice.

Peace & Blessings,
Melissa

Journal Page

Journal Page

Journal Page

Journal Page

Journal Page

About The Author

Melissa Rivers is a Creative Peace Coach and owner of Origins of Peace, LLC. She uses her skills to coach individuals to think outside the box to add more peaceful moments in their lives, businesses, and relationships.

Melissa knew at a young age that God gifted her with a ministry of service to others. Her formula for life can be summed up in Romans 12:18 (NIV), which says, *"If it is possible, as far as it depends on you, live at peace with everyone."* As Melissa says, "This scripture can help individuals tap into their unrealized potential to achieve success through peaceful empowerment.

Oftentimes, women are not aware of their strength until strength is their only choice and at that point, we are too exhausted from hurt and grief to handle the test adequately.

To learn more about Melissa's work and to join her email list for notices regarding her lectures and events, visit her website: **www.originsofpeace.com**

Thank you for your support.